How to make a Paperweight

To introduce this gag you say: 'Ladies and gentlemen, I will now show you how to make a paperweight.'

You then pick up a newspaper from your table and place it on the floor, take two steps backwards and, with your finger pointing at the paper, say! 'Wait . . . wait!'

Funny Business contains dozens of quick gags, and comedy sketches, magic tricks and mind-boggling juggling routines to teach you all you need to know to become an accomplished comedian. With the help of this book you'll be the funniest entertainer around.

Also in Red Fox by Peter Eldin:

DIY Joke Book
Skool Graffitti
The Vampire Jokebook
Woolly Jumper Joke Book
Crazy Kites
Crazy Magic

FUNNY BUSINESS

Peter Eldin

Illustrated by Harry Venning

RED FOX

A Red Fox Book
Published by Arrow Books Limited
20 Vauxhall Bridge Road, London SW1V 2SA

An imprint of the Random Century Group

London Melbourne Sydney Auckland
Johannesburg and agencies throughout the world

Red Fox edition 1990

Text © Data Forum Ltd 1990

The right of Peter Eldin to be identified as the author of this work has been asserted by him in accordance with the Copyright, Designs and Patents Act, 1988.

This book is sold subject to the condition that it shall not, by way of trade or otherwise, be lent, resold, hired out, or otherwise circulated without the publisher's prior consent in any form of binding or cover other than that in which it is published and without a similar condition including this condition being imposed on the subsequent purchaser.

Set in Century Schoolbook
by JH Graphics Ltd, Reading

Made and printed in Great Britain by
Courier International, Tiptree, Essex

ISBN 0 09 970550 8

CONTENTS

Introduction

Quick Gags
How to make a paperweight	15
Joan of Arc impression	16
Shakespeare impression	16
Bacon impression	16
Left-handed soldier	16
The lost aeroplane	17
Oink! Oink!	17
A pain in the neck	18
Creature from outer space	18
Take me to your leader	18
There's a frog in my throat	19
A toast	19
The singer	19
Shaving mirror	20
Pig tear	20

I Say, I Say, I Say
Kate and Sydney	21
The sun	22
I'm in love with an elephant	22
Socks	23

Two's Company
Stamp collection	24
The President's finger	24

Meetings	25
Aaargh!	26
Answer the phone	27
The brush-off	27
Feeling bored	27
You don't say	28
Travelling moustache	28
Learner lover	29

Sketches

Two minds as one	31
This is your life	34

Actions Speak Louder . . .

Have a good trip	40
Doing the splits	41
A swinging hit	42
Arm stretch	44
Hand stand	44
Fantastic fingers	44
Give it a twist	46
Charleston crossover	48
Off and on	50

For my next trick

Bang-gone	51
Floating on air	52
Dead correct	54
You're right, baby!	55
Duck or rabbit?	56
Half a card	57
It must be mindreading	59
That's right!	59
One at a time	59
All together	60

That's torn it	60
That takes the biscuit	61
Vanishing biscuit	62
The amazing vanishing magician	62
Three-way production	63

Jokey Juggling

Going for a spin	65
Hat spin	66
Jumping hat	68
Travelling hoop	69
Going on a journey	70
Hat flip	70
The animated hat	72
Hat hang-up	73
Coat hanger hang-up	74
Coat return	74
Coat folding	75

Clowning Around

Put on a happy face	76
Pom pom hat	77
Bow tie	79
Wet William	80
The growing man	81
The catcher caught	83
The thing	84
Flower power	85
Button up	87
Three legs are better than two	87
A glass of milk	88
Glass of water gag	90
Tail seat	90

Comedy Props

Toothless comb	92

Big head	93
Ear, ear	93
Spot the spider	94
Coat hanger discomfort	95
Sock it to 'em	95
The missing finger	95
Long arms	96
Matching handkerchief	97
Pull your socks up	97
Beads of perspiration	98
Bouncing handkerchief	98
A splitting headache	100
Banana split	101
Light-headed	102
Ball point	103
The injured finger	104
Autoclapper	105
Playing cards	106
The eyes have it	107

INTRODUCTION

Everyone enjoys a good laugh. Everyone likes a good comedian. You can be that comedian — with a little help from *Funny Business*. It is great fun to be able to make people laugh. This book will show you how for it is packed with jokey ideas you can use for the hilarious entertainment of your family and friends.

You may have heard the expression 'Comedy is a serious business'. That is certainly true if you plan to put on any type of comedy act.

It is important that you gain the attention of the audience right at the start of the act. It is also equally important to maintain that interest right through to the end.

One problem faced by all new performers is the difficulty of finding suitable material for the act. Some clever people can actually make up, and then perform, their own material but most of us have to get it from books or buy it from the clever people who thought it up in the first place. You should be able to find enough funny ideas in this book to keep you going for quite a long time.

Whatever material you use, always try to mould it to your own personality. *You* are the most important part of your act. The material you use takes second place to you — but it should still be as good as you can make it.

Moulding material to your own personality is a difficult thing to do. It can take a long time to do it properly, but during that time you will be constantly learning how to present your act to the best advantage.

If you want to become a good performer do not expect to achieve perfection overnight. Most professional entertainers have undergone many years of hard work before they become well known.

You, of course, may not wish to become a professional entertainer but just want to do a few funny things to amuse your friends. Even so, you should still choose your material with care, practise it thoroughly, and present it professionally.

In this book there are lots of comedy ideas and gags. But when you come to put some of them together into an act you must think about what you are doing. The items you select and the order you present them are both important factors.

Putting together an act in the correct sequence is called 'routining' and there are many theories as to the best way to do this. However, there is only one rule that applies to every theory and that is that you must start with something interesting; you must finish with something interesting and you must put something interesting in between.

If you change that to 'something interesting and funny' then you have the basis of a comedy act. Unfortunately, it is not quite as simple as it sounds!

The comedy act

Let us break down a comic act into five parts and see how they should be planned, and how the various parts combine to form the whole.

Part one is the opening item. It has to get the audience's attention. Some performers have said that if you do not 'grab' the audience within the first ten seconds of your appearance then you have lost them for the rest of the act.

So, for your first item choose something that is fast, colourful and original. Fast, because the audience wants something to make them continue watching; colourful, to gain their attention; and original, to give the impression you are worth watching.

Part two can slow the pace down a little but should not be too long-winded.

Part three, which is the middle part of the act, can be the longest of the five parts.

Part four has to keep the interest created by the first three parts and carry the audience into the final part of the act. As far as possible part four should be bright, lively and preferably original.

Part five has to be something that will cause the audience to remember your act. For a comedy act it should be something that keeps them laughing even after you have left the stage.

Almost all acts, even the individual gags and sketches, can be broken down in this way. It should be pointed out, however, that although five points have been described above it is not always necessary to have all five elements. Sometimes, especially with a quick gag, there could be just the first element. At other times there could be more than five elements.

Bang-Gone on page 00 can be regarded as six elements. These are:

1. The lie that the balloon is solid.
2. Banging the balloon on the table to 'prove' it is solid.
3. Covering the balloon with the scarf.
4. Removing the pin from your lapel — which builds up audience anticipation as to what is to happen next.
5. Bang!
6. The tag line that says it could have been a good trick.

Good comedy should appear to be unplanned and off the cuff. In actual fact, a lot of thought and planning must go into it to make it appear this way. Nothing should be left to chance — everything should be thought out and practised beforehand.

You should always plan out and rehearse your act before performing it. Think about what you are going to say and how you are going to say it. If you are going to use any props of any sort, make sure you know where they will be and what you are going to do with them when you have finished with them. You should also rehearse any movements you make so you don't accidentally get tangled up in any scenery or fall over your props (unless, of course, you have planned it that way to get extra laughs).

Above all else – keep your act short. Remember the old show business saying: 'Leave 'em wanting more!'

QUICK GAGS

How to make a paperweight

To introduce this gag you say: 'Ladies and gentlemen, I will now show you how to make a paperweight.'

You then pick up a newspaper from your table and place it on the floor, take two steps backwards and, with your finger pointing at the paper, say: 'Wait . . . wait!'

Joan of Arc impression

Introduce this gag by saying: 'Ladies and gentlemen, I would now like to give you my impression of Joan of Arc.'

Then put your hands behind your back and blow down around your feet as if putting out the flames of a fire!

Shakespeare impression

This is a very quick joke. You say: 'My impression of Shakespeare.'

Then you pick up a spear and shake it!

Bacon impression

This is a follow-up to the Shakespeare impression.

Mention the fact that there is a theory that some of Shakespeare's plays were really written by Bacon. You then say: 'And here he is,' as you lift a rasher of bacon up from your table.

Left-handed soldier

For an impression of a left-handed soldier all you have to do is bring your left hand up to your right temple in a salute.

It may not sound like much but it does really look very funny.

The lost aeroplane

Announce that you are going to do an impression of an aeroplane that is lost.

Then spread your arms out, like wings, and move around the stage making a noise like an aeroplane engine. Make sure you 'bank' your wings every time you do a turn. All the time you are doing this, keep looking down for a suitable place to land.

As you come to realize that you are lost, gradually change the sound of the engine noise into crying!

Oink! Oink!

This is how to do an impression of a walrus:

Take two pencils and tuck them under your upper lip as shown.

Place your hands back to back and clap them together, and make the noise: 'Oink, oink, oink!'

A pain in the neck

To do an impression of Dracula, put two pencils under your upper lip, as you did for the **Walrus Impression,** and go: 'Aaargh!'

You can then say something like: 'That's enough of Dracula – he's just a pain in the neck.'

Creature from outer space

Announce that you are about to do an impression of an alien space creature cleaning his glasses.

Then remove an imaginary pair of glasses and mime the action of cleaning the first lens, then the second lens . . . then the third lens . . . then the fourth lens . . . and keep on cleaning imaginary lenses until your audience gets the joke.

Take me to your leader

This is another impression of a creature from outer space.

Pick up any two objects and place them against each side of your head and say: 'Take me to your leader.'

It does not really matter what objects you use for this gag. Two whisks look very funny, but you could also use forks, glasses, light bulbs, metal springs, spoons . . . in fact, almost anything that is to hand.

There's a frog in my throat

As you are talking, make your voice suddenly go rather hoarse. Then cough a few times and say: 'Excuse me, I've got a frog in my throat.'

As you say this, reach up to your mouth and apparently remove a small frog. After that your voice is fine.

Of course, the frog isn't real – it is simply a small toy frog that you have had hidden in your hand all the time.

A toast

Raise a wine glass to the audience and say: 'Ladies and gentlemen, I would now like to give you a toast.'

Then reach into your pocket and take out a slice of toast. Make sure everyone sees it and then throw it into the audience!

The singer

Announce that you are going to sing a song.

Before you start singing, take two balls of cotton wool and put them in your ears.

When the laughter has finished, say (as if explaining your action): 'I've heard it before!' And you should get another laugh.

The same gag can be used if you play an instrument in your act.

Shaving mirror

Pick up a hairbrush from your table and look at it as if you are gazing into a hand mirror.

Then say: 'Goodness! I need a shave!'

(This gag is not recommended for girls! Girls should say: 'Oh, my hair is a mess!')

Pig tear

You show your audience a sheet of paper and claim to be an expert paper tearer.

You then fold the paper and start tearing little bits from it as you announce: 'I will show you how I can tear out the shape of a pig.'

Continue tearing bits from the paper, allowing the pieces to flutter to the floor, until there is nothing left in your hands.

Look at the audience apologetically as you say: 'Well, I didn't make a pig.'

Look down at the mess on the floor. Then look up and smile as you say: 'But at least I made a litter!'

I SAY, I SAY, I SAY

In the days when music hall comedians used to tour the theatres of Great Britain, monologues were extremely popular.

The word 'monologue' actually means a speech delivered by one person, but the monologues of the music hall were more than just speeches, they were comedy interludes, often accompanied by a pianist. Today, the monologue is considered rather old-fashioned but it can still get laughs if performed correctly.

Kate and Sydney

This should be performed as a boy using a high-pitched voice. You should also give the impression of being a little shy.

> My name is Sydney,
> And I'm in love with Kate.
> We're going to be married,
> I really cannot wait;
> For, when we're together she and I,
> We will make a Kate and Sydney pie!

The sun

It warms us up.
It gives us light.
If it were not for the sun
Every warm day
     – would be a cold night!

I'm in love with an elephant

I'm in love with an elephant
And she's in love with me.
We met at two
     – in the local zoo,
And had a cup of tea.

We got engaged on the fifth of May
And drank champagne all night.
She got so drunk
     – it shrivelled her trunk
It was such a funny sight.

I'm in love with an elephant
And she's in love with me.
We're so in love
     – we're like turtle doves
Billing and cooing in a tree.

We're getting married one day in June
The vicar's practising his verse.
As we walk down the aisle
     – we'll wear a big smile
For the wedding car's a broken-down hearse.

Socks

Socks smell.
Socks get holes in them.
Socks are such useless things.
Why don't we do away with them . . .
and paint our legs lots of pretty colours instead?

TWO'S COMPANY

Stamp collection

As your partner is talking on stage, you walk on and ask him: 'Do you collect stamps?'

Your partner replies: 'Yes, I do.'

You then stamp on his foot (you actually stamp on the ground near the foot) and say: 'Well, there's one for your collection.'

Then you walk off, leaving your partner hopping around on one foot!

The President's finger?'

You wiggle your little finger and say to your partner: 'Did you know that the American president cannot wiggle that finger?'

'No. Why is that?' your partner replies.

'Because it is mine!'

You do not of course have to use the American president for this gag — it can be anyone who is well known to your audience.

Meetings

To introduce this gag, you mention to the audience the fact that when people meet, their actions depend upon what sort of job they do. You and your partner then demonstrate some examples.

Here are a few suggestions you can try – but try to think up some of your own ideas as well.

Two mind-readers meeting:

You and your partner approach each other from either side of the stage. You shake hands and you say: 'You are fine. How am I?' to which your partner replies: 'You are feeling great.' Both walk off stage.

Two doctors meeting:

You and your partner approach and take each other's pulse. Then you both pause, while counting the pulse, and say: 'Mmmm.' You both then place a thermometer in the other's mouth and walk off stage.

Two ballet dancers meeting:

You both dance on stage, perform a pas-de-deux together, and then leap off.

Two television sports-presenters meeting:

You both walk up to each other and shake hands. One of you says: 'I think we should see an action replay of that.'

So you walk backwards off stage and then come on again and shake hands.

This time the other presenter says: 'Let's take a look at that in slow motion.'

Once again you both walk backwards off stage and then come on again. This time you approach and shake hands as before but all your actions are in slow motion!

Aaargh!

One partner is on stage as the other approaches, wearing a hideous mask.

The first partner appears not to notice but just says 'Hello' and carries on talking.

The second partner turns to face the first but there is still no reaction. He even tries tapping the first performer on the shoulder to get his attention but the first partner just tells him to stop being so annoying – and carries on talking.

This causes the second partner to give up. He removes the mask — and the sight causes the first partner to scream as if he had seen a horrible monster!

Answer the phone

Here is a quick gag for two:
A: 'Answer the phone.'
B: 'What?'
A: 'Answer the phone.'
B: 'But it's not ringing!'
A: 'Do you have to leave everything to the last minute?'

The brush-off

The first performer notices that his colleague's jacket is a little dusty and offers to brush it.

The second performer stands side-on to the audience as the first takes a clothes brush and begins brushing down the front of his friend's jacket.

As he moves round his friend, continually brushing, the first performer changes hands. He is now brushing his own coat and simply running his empty hand down his friend's jacket.

The audience will laugh when they see this but the second performer has no idea what all the merriment is about.

Feeling bored

One performer picks up a plank of wood and starts stroking it.

'What are you doing?' asks his partner.

'I'm feeling a little bored (board),' replies the first.

You don't say

During your act a telephone rings. You pick it up and say: 'Hello . . . You don't say . . . You don't say . . . You don't say!'

Then put the telephone down and your colleague asks: 'Who was that?' to which you reply: 'He didn't say!'

Travelling moustache

This gag involves a boy and a girl. The boy performer, who has a moustache, is talking to the audience when the girl walks on stage. He decides to kiss her.

When the kiss is over the audience will roar with laughter for the boy is now clean shaven and the girl, who is walking off stage, is wearing a moustache!

There are various ways of making a false moustache for this gag. The easiest is to attach a small wire to the bottom of the moustache. The moustache is attached to the boy's upper lip with sticky tape. When the girl kisses him she grips the wire between her teeth and holds it there as she walks off.

Learner lover

The first performer is on stage talking when his partner walks on, carrying a large envelope.

The partner says: 'Do you know a blonde called Gladys?'

'Yes, I do,' the first performer replies.

'Did you meet her behind the bike sheds yesterday evening?'

'Well, it's none of your business but, yes, I did as a matter of fact.'

'And did you give her a kiss?'

This causes the performer to blush a little but he admits that he did kiss the girl.

The partner then hands the performer the envelope, saying, 'Well, you must be the fellow she meant. She asked me to give you this.'

'Ah, it must be that photograph she promised me,' says the performer as he opens the envelope.

When he removes the contents the performer receives quite a surprise.

It is not the photograph he expected but a card on which there is a large red 'L', like that used for learner drivers!

SKETCHES

Two minds as one

This is a comedy mind-reading sketch for two people. One plays the mind-reader and the other the presenter. There is no need to use all of this act. You can add or subtract from it as you wish.

PRESENTER: Ladies and gentlemen, I would now like to introduce you to the greatest wonder of the age, someone who has honed his mind to perfection, the world's greatest mind-reader — The Great Mento!

(The Great Mento comes on stage and takes a bow. He (or she) is then blindfolded and the presenter goes down into the audience to borrow items from the spectators.)

PRESENTER: What is this? Please *coin*centrate.

MIND-READER: It's a coin.

PRESENTER: Fantastic! Can you tell me it's value? I will give you just *five* chances.

MIND-READER: It's a five-pence piece.

PRESENTER: (Looking at coin) Correct. Now can you tell me the date?

MIND-READER: It's the 22nd February, 1992 (or whatever date the performance might be).

PRESENTER: (Holds up a box of matches and shakes them vigorously) What have I here?

MIND-READER: Maraccas.

PRESENTER: No. I think you've met your *match* on this one.

MIND-READER: A match!

PRESENTER: No. I'll give you one more try and I'll *box* your ears if you don't get it right this time.

MIND-READER: A box of ears!

PRESENTER: (Frustratedly) Strike a light!

MIND-READER: A box of matches!

PRESENTER: Thank goodness for that! I am now looking at something on this lady's wrist. Take your *time* on this one.

MIND-READER: It's a watch.

PRESENTER: And can you tell me what this lady has on her finger?

MIND-READER: A ring.

PRESENTER: That is incredible. What type of ring is this married lady wearing?

MIND-READER: A wedding ring.

PRESENTER: Isn't that sensational?

PRESENTER: I am with a gentleman. Can you please tell me what he has on his head?

MIND-READER: Hair?

PRESENTER: Isn't that fantastic! Once again you are absolutely correct.

PRESENTER: I am holding a handkerchief. Can you please tell me what colour it is?

MIND-READER: Red.

PRESENTER: No. Concentrate and you will get it *white*.

MIND-READER: White.

PRESENTER: Correct, once again!

PRESENTER: I am now shuffling a pack of cards (he removes a pack of cards from his pocket and gives them a good mix) and I am going to remove one card. (He does so.) Can you tell me the name of the card?

MIND-READER: Charlie.

PRESENTER: No, can you tell what card I have picked?

MIND-READER: (names any card)

PRESENTER: Absolutely correct. (*He does not show the audience the card but simply replaces it in the pack.*)

PRESENTER: (He then takes the Two of Clubs from the pack and shows it to the audience.) I have taken another card from the pack. I want you *to* tell me its value.

MIND-READER: I think it's a two.

PRESENTER: Fantastic! And can you tell me the suit . . . I'll *club* you if you do not get this right.

MIND-READER: A club! The card you are holding is the Two of Clubs.

PRESENTER: (*Writes the figure 7 on a board*). Can you tell me what number I have written?

MIND-READER: Four.

PRESENTER: (*Turns board over and adds another stroke to make the upside-down 7 into a 4.*) Absolutely correct! Ladies and gentlemen, isn't he fantastic! The incredible Great Mento.

The mind-reader then whisks off his blindfold and the two take a bow.

This is your life

You need a minimum of three characters for this sketch. Two are on stage all the time and the third can play all the other parts as only one of them is on stage at any time. Alternatively, you can have different people playing the various parts.

The main character, Michael Asprin, has rather a lot to say but this can be written down in the book he is holding so he doesn't have to learn his part word for word.

If you have music available you could start this sketch with the music from the television show *This Is Your Life*. It is a good idea to distort the music a little to make it sound funny. If recorded music or actual musicians are not available you could get some of your friends to pretend to be an orchestra playing this famous signature tune.

In the opening scene, Noah Lott, a schoolmaster, is addressing a class. (Don't worry — you do not need to employ lots of pupils for this sketch. If the teacher is standing at a blackboard teaching an imaginary classroom the audience will understand what is happening.)

The famous television interviewer, Michael Asprin, comes on carrying a large red book on which is written *This Is Your Life*. He is wearing the disguise of a mortar board and a teacher's black gown, both of which are far too big for him. He also has a large, obviously false, moustache.

MICHAEL ASPRIN: (to the audience) Good evening, Ladies and Gentlemen. Our subject tonight is a man who has devoted his life to educating children whether they like it or not. I hope this brilliant disguise of mine will work and that I can persuade this gentleman to be our victim . . . I mean, guest . . . for tonight. (He creeps across the stage to Noah Lott.) I am sorry to interrupt your lesson, I'm sure your pupils are finding it very interesting.
PUPILS: (played by some of your friends off stage) Oh, no we're not.
NOAH LOTT: Oh, yes you are.

PUPILS: (Louder) Oh, no we're not.

NOAH LOTT: (Louder, still) Oh, yes you are. (This can be repeated for as long as it is getting laughs. Eventually, the teacher yells 'Shut up! ! !' at the top of his voice).

MICHAEL ASPRIN: (Removing disguise) Tonight, Noah Lott, wit, racoon . . . sorry, rancontuer, sage . . . and onion, educationalist, and star of the local job centre. Tonight, this is your life.

NOAH LOTT: Goodness gracious — I don't believe it.

MICHAEL ASPRIN: (Opens the large book) Yes, tonight this is your life. And what a fascinating life it has been. You were born at a very early age . . . but your parents were rather disappointed. They wanted a child. And here's someone who means a great deal to you.

MONA LOTT: (Off stage) Yes, Noah, baby. Many's the time I've powdered your bottom. When I changed your nappy I always used to say: 'A bit of talcum is always walcum.'

(Mona Lott comes on stage and gives Noah a cuddle)

NOAH LOTT: Hallo, mumsy.

MICHAEL ASPRIN: I understand that things were bad when Noah was born.

MONA LOTT: Oh, yes. We were very poor. We were so poor we couldn't afford coal for a fire. So Noah's dad used to suck a peppermint and we'd all warm our hands around his tongue.

(Mona Lott walks off stage)

MICHAEL ASPRIN: Thank you Mona Lott. Do you have any memories of those days, Noah?

NOAH LOTT: Yes, I particularly remember my first day at school. We were so poor Mum couldn't afford to buy me any shoes ... so I blackened my feet and laced my toes together.

MICHAEL ASPRIN: After you were thrown out ... after you left school, you joined the army where you met someone who greatly influenced your life.

MAJOR RODAHED: (Off stage) I was the man who was responsible for Noah Lott becoming a teacher.

MICHAEL ASPRIN: Yes, It's your old army chum, Major Rodahed.

(The major enters and proffers his right hand as Noah gets up from his seat with his right hand forward to shake hands. Unfortunately, the major holds his hand high and Noah holds his low. They then change positions to try again — but this time the major puts his hand low and Noah puts his high. You can do this a couple more times before both people decide to give up.)

MICHAEL ASPRIN: Tell me how you started Noah Lott's career.

MAJOR RODAHED: Well, one day Noah saw a sign outside the police station which said: 'Murderer Wanted' ... and he went in and applied for the job ... As soon as I heard about it I realized he was as thick as the school gravy so I suggested he become a teacher. And he's never looked back since. He daren't look back ... the police are still after him. (Walks off stage)

MICHAEL ASPRIN: You then went to America to study. Did you enjoy that?

NOAH LOTT: Not very much ... I couldn't speak the language.

MICHAEL ASPRIN: When you returned to Britain you met another man who was to have a great

impact on your life; the night watchman at the dischewed . . . disused toffee works in Nurglers Road . . . your old friend Sidney Shorthouse.
(Sidney Shorthouse, an old man in a dirty overall, enters. He takes two spoons from his pocket and starts to play them. Michael Asprin stops him and the spoons fall to the floor. A second later a large number of other spoons fall from Sidney's overall.)

MICHAEL ASPRIN: I'm sorry, Mr Shortmouse but you can't play the spoons in here.

SIDNEY SHORTHOUSE: Shorthouse! And why can't I play the spoons? This is *Search For A Star* isn't it?

MICHAEL ASPRIN: No, Mr Shirthouse, it's *This Is Your Life*.

SIDNEY SHORTHOUSE: Shorthouse! Oh, what a surprise. It's a great honour to be chosen. You've certainly taken your time getting to me but I knew you would eventually.

MICHAEL ASPRIN: No, Mr Shortlouse . . .

SIDNEY SHORTHOUSE: Shorthouse!

MICHAEL ASPRIN: It's not *your* life. It's Noah Lott's life.

SIDNEY SHORTHOUSE: Who's he? I bet he's not as famous as me. You've brought me here under false pretences. I'll have the law on the lot of you. I know my rights. I'll complain to. . . . (A long hook comes from the wings and hauls him, still protesting, off stage.)

MICHAEL ASPRIN: Thank you, Mr Shoothouse.

SIDNEY SHORTHOUSE: (Off stage) Shorthouse!!

MICHAEL ASPRIN: It seems only fitting that we should finish this tribute to your life as a teacher with an appreciation from one of your pupils. Unfortunately, we couldn't find one who appreciated you . . . but eventually one was forced . . . one volunteered to come along. She lives over a quarter of a mile away but tonight we have flown her here, at great expense, to be with you tonight. Your brightest pupil, Wanda Why.

(Wanda Why, in schoolgirl uniform and wearing long pigtails, enters and curtseys. She then stands swinging her arms nervously. Michael Asprin watches this for a while and then, unable to stand it any longer, grasps her hand — whereupon his hand begins to swing in time with the girl's. Eventually, he manages to break free.)

MICHAEL ASPRIN: What do you think of this great man?

WANDA WHY: I think he likes me . . . because he puts lots of kisses against my sums.

MICHAEL ASPRIN: (As Wanda walks off stage) Thank you, Wanda. (Hands the book to Noah Lott) Noah Lott, this is your life . . . and to finish, a special tribute from your pupils . . .

(Lots of wet flannels are thrown at Noah Lott from off stage accompanied by boos and catcalls. Michael Asprin and Noah Lott rush off stage as the *This Is Your Life* music is played again.)

ACTIONS SPEAK LOUDER...

Have a good trip

As you are walking from one side of the stage to the other, you suddenly trip over an imaginary object.

You look back to see what caused you to trip, and then bend down and pretend to smooth out the surface of the floor – as if there had been a bump in it.

You walk forward again – only to trip over something else!

To do the 'trip', all you have to do is to hit the instep of your right foot against the arch of your left foot, then lurch your body forward a little. With practice, this movement can look really convincing.

instep of left foot hits against heel of right foot

Doing the splits

Announce that you are going to do the splits (going down to the floor from a standing position by sliding your legs out on each side).

You stand with your legs apart and then slide them further apart, allowing your body to move towards the floor. After a short while (well before you reach the floor!) you stop, stand up again and say: 'Half today . . . and half tomorrow.'

Like many of the items in this book, it does not sound particularly funny in print. But just try it in front of an audience and you will discover that it always raises a laugh.

A swinging hit

As you are talking to your audience, your right arm suddenly sticks out as shown.

You do not notice this for a while. When you do see it, just take a quick look and carry on talking.

Slowly it dawns on you that your arm has taken on a strange position. Stop talking and slowly turn your head to look at the arm. Look at the audience with a puzzled expression on your face, then look back at the arm.

Now tap the right hand with your left. The right hand swings loosely from side to side, like a pendulum, and then gradually stops.

Tap the right hand a little harder so the right arm swings even more this time.

You decide that this is a good bit of fun so you now give your right hand a really hard tap.

This time the arm swings so much it goes around in a complete circle and your right hand slaps you on the head!

Stagger around as if in a daze for a few seconds then, when the laughter has died down, go on to another gag.

Arm stretch

You will need to wear a jacket for this amusing stunt.

Hold your left arm across the front of your body. Press your coat sleeve against your body to keep it still.

Then, with your right hand, give your left hand several tugs towards the right. It looks as though you are stretching your left arm!

Hand stand

Announce that you are going to perform a difficult acrobatic stunt – you are going to stand on your hands.

Get ready, as if you are actually going to do a hand stand. Act as though you are just about to do it, several times, but each time change your mind.

Eventually, you announce the acrobatic feat one more time: 'Ladies and gentlemen, I am now going to stand on my hands.'

Then crouch down, place your hands on the floor and put your feet on them. You are standing on your hands!

Fantastic fingers

Announce that you are going to show an amazing feat of magic.

Close both hands into fists but leave the right forefinger extended. Hold the hands so your knuckles are pointing to the floor.

Now hit the side of the left hand with your right hand. As you do so, curl in your right forefinger and extend the left forefinger. Immediately bring your hands apart.

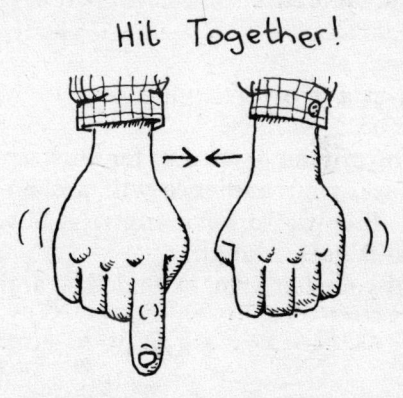

Hit Together!

Now do exactly the same in reverse — hit the fists together, close the left forefinger, extend the right forefinger and bring the hands apart again.

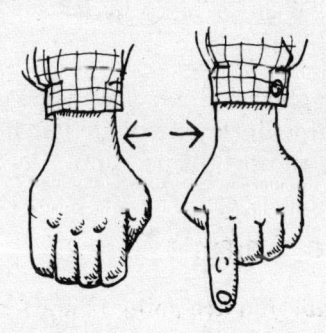

Forefinger travels from right hand to left!!

It looks as if you are transferring a finger from one hand to the other!

It is very unlikely that anyone will actually be fooled by your amazing feat of magic – but it will amuse your audience.

Give it a twist

There is no rhyme or reason for this strange action. In fact, your audience will probably think you are rather weird for doing it – but it looks funny and it gets a laugh.

Hold out your left arm, extended straight out to the left.

right hand taps inner elbow

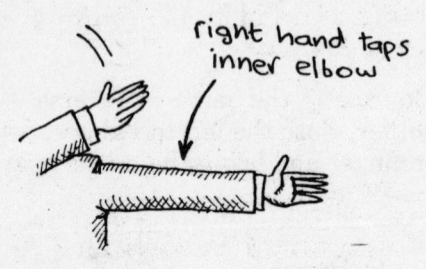

With your right hand, tap the inside of your left elbow and immediately lift your left hand so the forearm is in an upright position.

Left hand moves to upright

Next hit the back of your left hand causing it to move to a horizontal position with the fingers pointing towards your head.

Right hand taps back of left hand

Now turn the left hand to the left so the fingers are pointing away from you. Make a creaking noise as you do this.

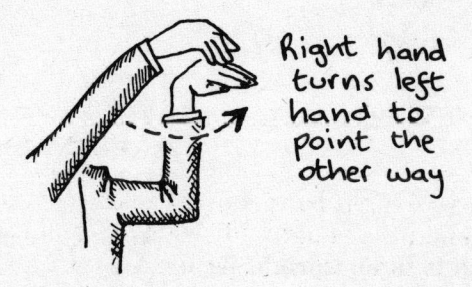

Right hand turns left hand to point the other way

It doesn't sound very funny in print – but try it in front of a mirror and you will see how strange it looks.

Charleston crossover

Although this movement has been around for over seventy years and is rather well known, it is very difficult to describe in words.

If you follow the description as you look at the diagrams you should get it right.

Stand with your legs apart. Bend down a little and place your right hand on your right knee and your left hand on the left knee.

① left hand on left knee, right hand on right knee. Knees apart.

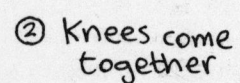

② Knees come together

Bend your knees and open your legs. Now bring the knees together and allow your left hand to move across to the right knee at the same time as the right hand goes on to the left knee. Open your legs again and your arms will be crossed.

Close the knees together and open them again, once again changing the hands from one knee to the other so you are back to the starting position.

Repeat all the actions quickly a few more times – or until you get fed up with it!

③ Right hand slides to left knee, left hand slides to right knee.

④ Knees apart and arms are crossed.

Reverse action, repeat several times.

Off and on

This takes a bit of practice but looks very clever when done properly.

Allow your jacket to slip down off your right arm.

With your left arm, swing the coat around behind your back and then to the front. As it reaches the front, allow the coat to fall from your left arm as you take it in your right hand.

Immediately put your right arm into the sleeve.

Continue to bring the coat around behind you so you can put your left hand into the other sleeve — and you have got the coat back on again.

For the best effect, try to do this all in one continuous movement.

FOR MY NEXT TRICK

Bang-gone

You show the audience an inflated balloon and say: 'Ladies and gentlemen, I have here a solid wooden ball.'

This obvious lie will certainly raise a few smiles and get everyone interested in what you are going to do.

'To prove it is solid I will bang it on the table.' As you tap the balloon on the table a few times you kick the table leg each time to produce the noise of a solid ball hitting the table.

The 'solid wooden ball' is then covered with a scarf.

You take a pin from your lapel as you announce: 'The amazing disappearance of a solid wooden ball.'

Place the pin under the scarf and burst the balloon.

As bits of rubber fall to the floor, whisk the scarf away with a dramatic flourish.

Rather surprised at the fact that your fantastic magic received laughter instead of applause you say: 'Don't laugh. If I could get rid of that bang I'd have a good trick, there!'

Floating on air

This amusing trick is very old and quite well known, but it still gets a laugh. In it, the magician tries to hypnotise his assistant but ends up in a trance himself. The assistant then makes the magician float in the air — but it is not long before the audience finds out how they have been deceived.

The magician announces that he is going to hypnotise his assistant. From his pocket he removes a watch on a chain. The watch is swung to and fro and the assistant is asked to concentrate upon it.

But the assistant keeps his head perfectly still and the magician's head is moved from side to side, watching the movement of the watch.

'You are going to sleep . . . to sleep . . . to sleep.' says the magician. But it is the magician who gradually closes his eyes and falls asleep!

The assistant takes the watch and leads the magician to a long bench at the rear of the stage. At the assistant's word of command the magician sits on the bench.

The assistant then lifts the magician's legs and

places them on the bench so he is now sideways on to the audience and sitting upright.

Next the assistant commands the magician to lie down on the bench.

Now the assistant picks up a large sheet from the floor in front of the bench and uses it to cover the magician's body.

As soon as he is out of sight the magician reaches down behind the bench and picks up two broom poles with shoes attached to one end.

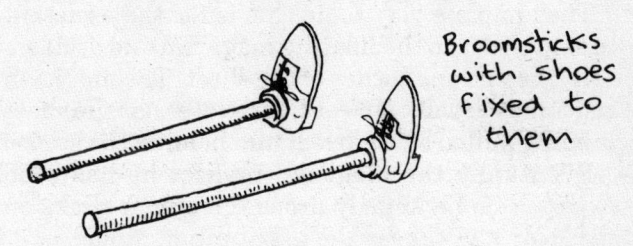

Broomsticks with shoes fixed to them

He then crouches down behind the bench with the broom poles held out in front of him. To make the broomsticks easier to carry, it is a good idea for the magician to tuck the ends under his arms as shown.

The assistant continues draping the sheet over the magician's body – or, at least, that is what the audience thinks. In fact, it is draped across the two poles and only the magician's head remains in view.

The magician rises slowly and then walks forward. It looks as if his body is floating on air.

At this point the magician could simply 'float' off stage. But if you want the audience to laugh you can 'accidentally' reveal how the floating is done.

The simplest way to do this is for the assistant to step closer to the floating magician and accidentally step on one corner of the sheet. The magician continues to walk forward, unaware that the sheet is being pulled off to reveal him holding the sticks!

Eventually the magician realizes he has been exposed. So he angrily drops the broom sticks on the floor and chases the assistant off stage.

Dead correct

Show an envelope to the audience and announce that it contains a picture of a famous person from the past.

Ask someone to name a famous person who has been dead for a long time. You can help by suggesting names, such as Shakespeare, Napoleon, Van Gogh, and so on.

A spectator gives you a name and you say: 'That is fantastic! Inside this envelope I have a picture of the very person you have just named!'

Then you pull the picture from the envelope. It is a picture of a skull!

'There you are,' you say, 'a picture of (named person) as he looks today!'

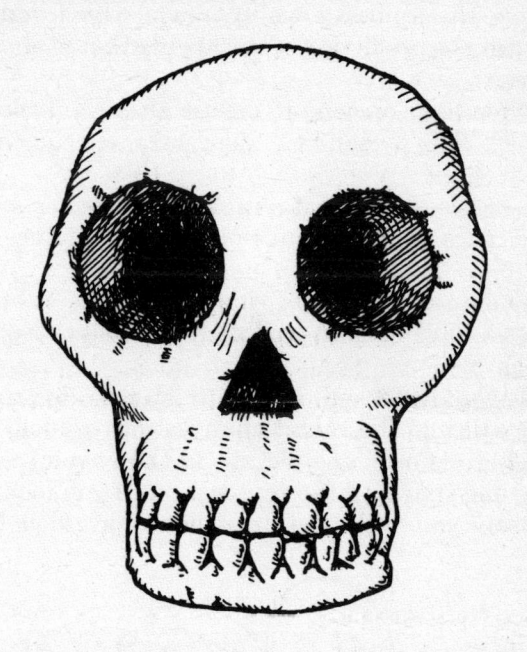

You're right, baby!

This gag is a variation of *Dead Correct*. Tell your audience that an envelope you are holding contains a picture of a famous person. Through the power of your mind you are going to get someone in the audience to name the person concerned.

Ask someone to name any famous person. When the name is called you pull the picture from the envelope. It is a drawing of a baby. 'There you are!' you say, 'a picture of (named person) – as a baby!'

Duck or rabbit?

Show the audience an envelope which you say contains a prediction of something that is about to happen.

Then ask someone to choose either a duck or a rabbit. The person has a perfectly free choice and may change his or her mind if they wish.

Let us suppose that a rabbit is chosen. You pull a picture from the envelope. It is a picture of a rabbit!

Then say: 'I'm glad you picked the rabbit. I would have been in trouble if you had chosen the duck.'

The audience will roar with laughter for, as you are talking, the rabbit changes into a duck!

There is only one picture in the envelope. It is the one shown in the illustration. If you look at it closely you will see that if held upright it looks like a rabbit — but if it is held sideways it looks like a duck.

So, whatever creature is chosen, all you have to do is bring the picture out from the envelope the correct way round to show that your prediction is correct.

The laughs come because you casually turn the picture around while you are talking and the audience realize how they have been tricked.

Half a card

Take a Nine of Diamonds from an old pack of cards and cut it as shown in the illustration.

Put this card in the top pocket of your jacket.

During your show ask someone to take a card from the pack.

For this trick you need the person to take the Five of Diamonds but you must seem to give him or her a fair choice. Magicians call this technique 'forcing' and here is one way you can force the Five of Diamonds.

Start off with the Five of Diamonds on top of the pack.

Ask someone to cut off any number of cards and place them on the table. (The Five of Diamonds will be the top card of this cut-off portion).

Pick up the rest of the cards and place them across the cut-off portion *as shown*.

Tell everyone that you are such an expert magician you will discover which card has been chosen.

You then realize that the person who cut the cards has not yet looked at one of them.

Lift off the top portion of the pack and ask the spectator to look at the card on the top of the bottom portion. (This is actually the Five of Diamonds you put on top of the pack at the start, but the spectator will think he has had a fair choice.)

Pull the card part way from your pocket and tell the spectator that this is his card.

He will say something like: 'No, that is the Nine of Diamonds. My card is the Five of Diamonds.'

You then pull the card right out of your pocket to show that it has only five diamonds on it!

It must be mind-reading

You will need an assistant to perform this act. Your assistant blindfolds you as you sit side on to the audience.

Your assistant then goes to one side of the stage and picks up various objects from a table. You describe each object accurately and the audience will be convinced that you possess some amazing mental ability.

You then turn to the audience and say: 'Wasn't that amazing!'

The spectators will then realize they have been had — for the blindfold is only over one eye so you could see everything that was going on!

This is because your assistant tied the blindfold over your eyes at an angle so only the eye nearest the audience was actually covered.

That's right!

Ask someone in the audience to think of any playing card.

Someone will name a card.

Then say: 'That's right!' and take a bow!

One at a time

You will need an assistant for this trick. Shuffle a pack of cards and then say to your assistant: 'Do you want them all together or one at a time?'

'One at a time,' says your assistant.

Then throw the cards, one at a time, at the assistant!

All together

This is used as a follow-up gag to *One at a time*.

Once again, shuffle a pack of cards and ask your assistant: 'Do you want them all together or one at a time?'

This time the assistant says: 'All together.'

So you throw the whole pack at him!

When doing this gag, the cards should be thrown so they miss the assistant. It is not so funny if someone gets hurt by a flying pack of cards.

That's torn it

Have a pack of cards shuffled, then spread out the cards on a table and ask a spectator to take any one card. Ask him to look at it and remember what it is.

Take the card back as you tell the audience about a magician you once saw. 'He had a card chosen and then he tore it into little pieces.' As you say this, tear the card into pieces.

Hand the spectator one piece as you say: 'He gave the spectator one piece and then he put all the other pieces in his left hand.' Put the pieces in your left hand.

'He then gave all the pieces a squeeze.' You squeeze the pieces.

'And when he opened his hand the card was completely restored.'

Open your hand. Look at the pieces. Throw them all in the air as you say: 'I wish I could do that trick!'

That takes the biscuit

Announce that you are going to perform a baffling magic trick. Show the audience a handkerchief and then hold one edge between the first and second fingers. The purpose of this is to spread the handkerchief out as wide as possible.

Next show the audience a biscuit and announce: 'Ladies and gentlemen . . . the incredible vanishing biscuit trick.'

Hold the handkerchief in front of the biscuit to hide it from view. Then bend down to put your face behind the handkerchief – and eat the biscuit!

You must make it obvious that you are eating the biscuit but at the same time you must give the impression that you are trying to do this without the audience knowing.

Come up from behind the handkerchief and then show the handkerchief on both sides. Amazing! The biscuit has vanished!

Some comedians would carry this gag a bit further by saying something after the biscuit has vanished but, because their mouth is full of biscuit, this is usually a bit messy!

Vanishing biscuit

Another biscuit vanishing trick – but this one is messy so only do it where the mess can be cleaned up easily.

Show the audience a biscuit in your right hand. Then place it in your left hand and close your hand around it.

Now squeeze your left hand in the same way that some magicians do when they make something disappear. As you do this you actually crumble the biscuit in your hand – allowing the crumbs to fall to the floor.

Open your left hand. The biscuit has vanished. Crumbs!

The amazing vanishing magician

Begin this trick by saying: 'For a very long time I have been working to develop a fantastic magical illusion – "The Amazing Vanishing Magician trick". Unfortunately, I have so far been able only to perfect half of this incredible feat but as it is so amazing I would like to show it to you. Ladies and gentlemen, the 'Amazing Vanishing Magician trick' – part one.

Then show the audience a large scarf which you hold between your hands at knee height. It is important that the bottom of the scarf touches the floor.

Now simply slip off your shoes and take one step backwards. The bottom edge of the scarf slides over the shoes to reveal them. As the shoes are empty it seems logical (doesn't it?) that the magician wearing them must have vanished!

Say: 'An incredible feat!' Emphasize the word 'feat' (feet) as you point to the empty shoes.

Allow the audience time to laugh, then throw the scarf off stage and slip your shoes back on again.

Three-way production

This has been called the **Three-Way Production** because there are at least three ways you can get your audience to laugh at the end.

The main part of the trick consists of the production of a wide variety of different objects from a hat on your table.

At the start of the trick the items you produce from the hat are similar to those produced by most magicians – a number of silk handkerchiefs, some flowers and a string of flags, for example. Every so often, however, produce something quite bizarre from the hat. These bizarre objects depend upon what you can dream up – an old boot, a string of sausages, a solid block of wood, a drainpipe, a tin of baked beans or perhaps a tortoise would all prove funny to your audience.

What the audience do not realize (although some of them may work it out after a while) is that there is a hole in both the hat and the table. Underneath the table, and concealed by the tablecloth, which reaches down to the floor, is your secret assistant who simply passes the production items up to you through the holes.

You now need a funny ending to the sequence. Here are three you can try. With a bit of thought you may be able to come up with some alternative ways to end the gag:

1. At the end of the production reach into the hat to get something else but pretend that there is nothing there. Try a few more times – but without success. Eventually, reach right into the hat (so your arm goes in well beyond the elbow) and bring up a hand – which is obviously the hand of the person hidden beneath the table.
2. At the end of the production look into the hat and let the audience know from your reactions that there is nothing there. Look again – a bit closer this time. There is still nothing there. Next look right into the hat – and a hand, wearing a boxing glove, will come out of the hat and punch you on the chin! You will, of course, have to practise this with your friend under the table to make sure you do not get hurt when doing this.
3. Reach into the hat for the last item but pretend it gets stuck. As you are struggling to remove it, allow the tablecloth to fall away – to reveal your secret confederate under the table!

JOKEY JUGGLING

Going for a spin

Your audience will be amazed by your juggling skill when you show this stunt.

Place a small ball on the open shade of a parasol or umbrella and keep the ball running around on the shade as you rotate the parasol.

Everyone will applaud your skill but will then have a good laugh when you take a bow. This is because you stop rotating the parasol and the ball is seen to be hanging by a thread!

Use a ping-pong ball and run a long thread through it and up to the tip of the parasol. Attach the thread to the top of the parasol with a drawing pin.

Provided you keep the parasol spinning, the ball will bounce around on the shade quite merrily. When you stop, allow the ball to hang down, revealing how the stunt was accomplished.

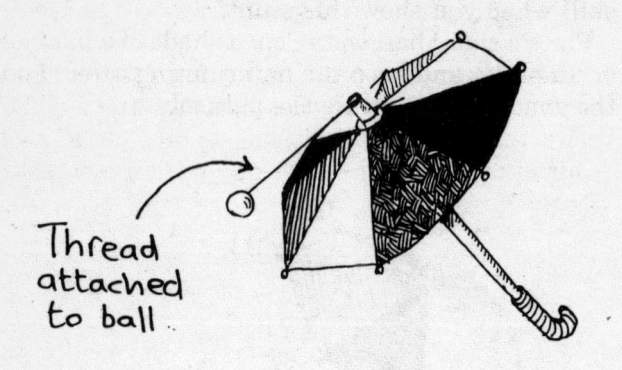

Thread attached to ball

Hat spin

Place a hat upside-down on your table and then put your right forefinger inside it.

If you are left-handed you may find that this trick works better using your left hand.

Move your forefinger in a circle around the inner part of the hat. Do this fast enough and you will find that you can lift your finger (still spinning, of course) and the hat will lift with it.

This works by centrifugal force — or is it centripetal force — or does it really matter? The main thing is that it works — and that it gives your audience the impression you are a talented juggler!

Jumping hat

When you place your hat on your head it jumps off – much to everyone's surprise and amusement.

All you have to do to accomplish this amusing stunt is tie a piece of elastic from one side of the hat brim to the other.

Elastic

It is as well to practise this stunt with hats of various sizes but, as a general rule, you will probably find that a hat that is slightly too big for you works best. With a large hat you can pull it down on to your head where it will stay wedged in position until you frown or make the top part of your head move.

Travelling hoop

This gag has to be worked on a stage, or somewhere with a screen on each side of the performing area. You will need two wooden hoops and two friends.

Show the audience a large wooden hoop and roll it across the stage. As you release the hoop, pull your hand down sharply. This will cause the hoop to spin so it will roll away and then come back to you. With practice you will be able to roll the hoop quite a long distance before it comes back.

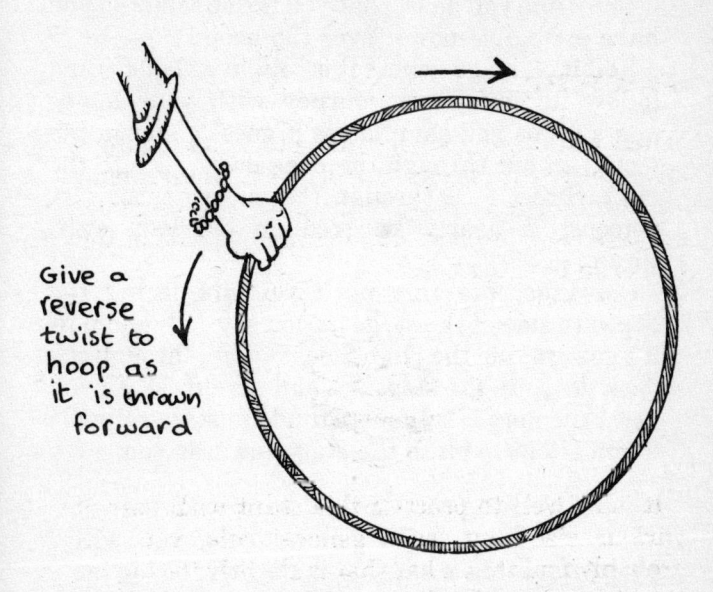

Give a reverse twist to hoop as it is thrown forward

Repeat this trick a few times but on the last roll, let the hoop go right off the stage. Stretch out your hand ready for the hoop's return, but instead of it rolling *back* to you it rolls on *behind* you, from the other side of the stage!

As the first hoop rolls off stage it is caught by your first friend. After a few seconds' pause your second friend rolls the second hoop on to the other side of the stage.

Going on a journey

This gag is worked in exactly the same way as **Travelling Hoop** but is presented differently.

This time you boast that you are so talented you have incredible power over the hoop.

Roll it off stage (where it is caught as before) and follow its imaginary journey with your hands and eyes as you say: 'There it goes . . . down the steps . . . out through the back door . . . into the High Street . . . through the supermarket . . . whoops! It nearly knocked an old lady over, there . . .'

Continue like this until you are facing the opposite side of the stage as you say: '. . . and now it's going along the High Street again, through the back door, up the steps . . . and here it is!' As you say: 'And here it is,' your second assistant rolls the duplicate hoop on to the stage towards you.

Hat flip

When you put on a hat it immediately leaps up in the air. You catch it and try putting it on your head again but again it flies off.

You can repeat this action as often as you like. To do it you have to hold the hat with your second fingers under the brim, *as shown*.

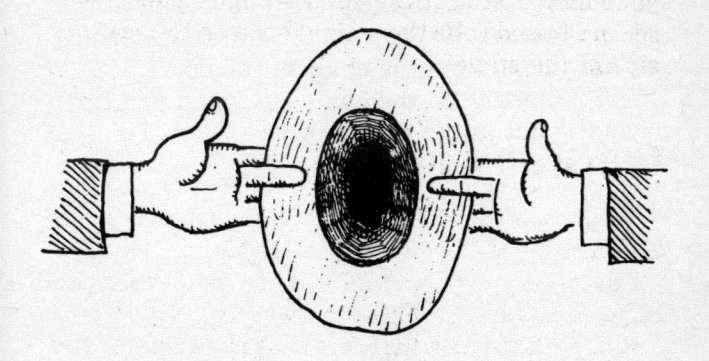

As you place the hat on your head the middle fingers flick the hat into the air.

The animated hat

When you make your entrance you are wearing a hat. You remove this and place it on a chair at the side of the stage. As you turn towards the audience the hat jumps from the chair to the floor.

You replace it on the chair but when you turn away the hat jumps off again.

Once again you put the hat back on the chair. This time you back away slowly, keeping your eye on the hat. Nothing happens... until you turn to face the audience and the hat jumps off yet again!

You can repeat this as many times as you like.

The gag works like this. Attached to the chair is a thread which runs off stage to an assistant.

When you put the hat on the chair you place it over the thread. If the assistant pulls sharply on the thread the hat will jump from the chair.

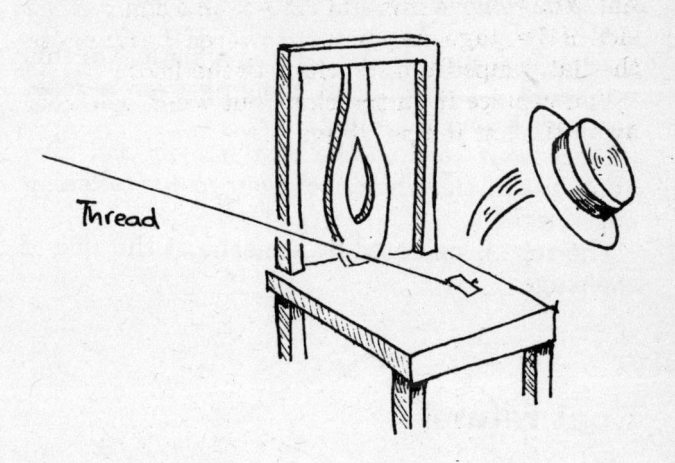

Hat hang-up

You enter wearing a hat. You take off your hat and try to hang it on part of the scenery but it falls to the floor.

Try to hang it a couple more times – but with the same result.

Then take a piece of chalk from your pocket and draw a hook on the scenery.

This time, when you hang it up, your hat hangs on the hook you have just drawn!

What the audience do not see is that there is a small nail in the scenery and it is this, not the chalk hook, that really holds your hat.

Coat hanger hang-up

When you are about to perform a particularly difficult juggling or acrobatic feat, remove your coat.

Then look up into the air and whistle. On this command a coat hanger, hanging from a rope, descends from the ceiling.

Place your coat on the coat hanger and give another whistle, whereupon your coat is taken up out of sight.

The rope is operated by someone at the side of the stage.

Coat return

This is best worked on a stage, or in a room where there are side screens.

Pretend that you are about to perform a particularly difficult juggling feat, and remove your coat and throw it off stage into the wings.

Turn to face the audience, ready to show your juggling skills, when the coat is thrown back by someone off stage!

This action is funny just by itself but if you and your off-stage assistant can manage to get the coat to land over your head, it can be even funnier as you stumble around the stage trying to get yourself out from under the coat.

Coat folding

Here is another gag you can use when you have to remove your coat.

Take off your coat and make a great point of folding it as neatly as you can.

Take your time over this, making sure all the folds are exactly as you want them, and that the coat is neat and tidy – then chuck it over your shoulder so it lands in a heap on the floor!

CLOWNING AROUND

Put on a happy face

There are two main types of clown make-up. One is known as the white-faced clown and the other is known as the auguste, which consists of red, white and black colours.

Professional clowns use greasepaint for their make-up but it is just as good to use make-up crayons you can buy from a toy shop.

The first stage in applying make-up is to wash your face! When your face is completely dry, comb your hair straight back — you want the make-up on your face, not on your hair.

Next put on some moisturising cream. This provides a protective barrier between your skin and the make-up. It also makes it easier to remove the make-up later.

Put a foundation cream or 'pancake' make-up all over your face and then dust it with powder.

If you are going to be a white-faced clown then use talcum powder as your foundation.

The rest of the make-up of a white-faced clown usually consists of red lips and black eyebrows.

The make-up of an auguste is much more over the top. The eyes and the mouth should be exaggerated with a thick black line around the outside. If you want the mouth to look happy curl the ends upwards; if you want to look sad then the mouth curves downwards. Fill in the mouth and eye area with brightly coloured greasepaint or lipstick. The traditional colours are red, white and black, because they are visible from a distance, but it is a good idea to experiment with different colours to see which you like best.

The nose can also be painted in a bright colour, or spots could be applied to make it look funny. An easier way is to buy a funny nose from a toy shop.

Always keep an eye on toy shops, joke shops and novelty shops for they will often have bits and pieces you can use in your clown act — false feet, funny hats, masks, and so on.

As a general rule, a clown's clothes are brightly coloured, and usually greatly exaggerated. If a clown wears a bow tie it will be incredibly large, the trousers will be baggy, the shoes ridiculously over-sized, and so on.

The clothes worn by a white-faced clown are usually rather smart, glamorous and often covered with sequins.

Jumble sales are a great place for buying clothes for your clown act that won't cost too much.

Pom pom hat

White-faced clowns often wear a conical-shaped white hat with pom poms on the front of it. You can make one quite easily from cardboard.

Cut out the shape shown from a sheet of white card. Now bend the shape round and glue the two edges together.

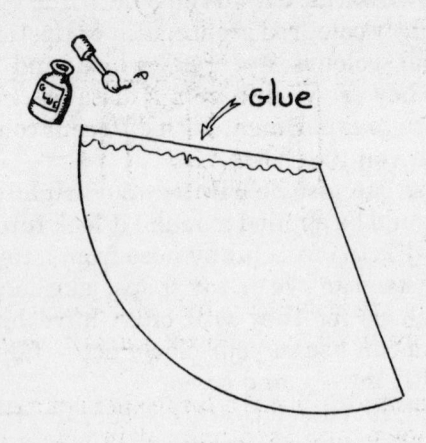

All you have to do now is stick some coloured pom poms or bows of ribbon on the front and the hat is complete.

Bow tie

A bow tie is a colourful item of clothing that can be worn by an auguste clown – and it is very easy to make.

All you need is to cut a large sheet of card to the shape shown, and then paint it in bright colours.

Attach a strip of wide elastic to the tie as shown. The elastic should be just long enough to go around your neck to hold the tie in place.

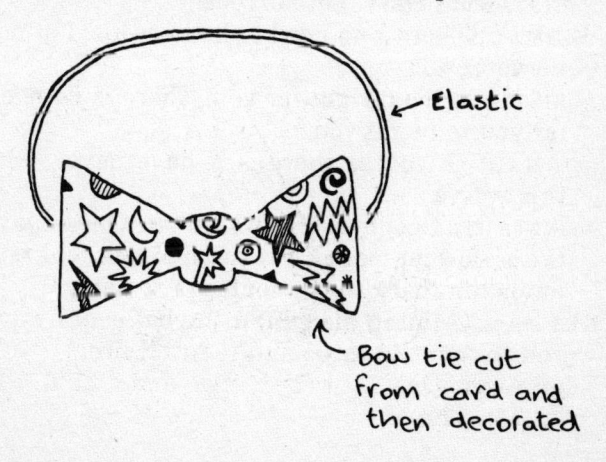

← Elastic

← Bow tie cut from card and then decorated

Wet William

This gag involves two people. One carries a large gun (which can be made quite easily from cardboard) and the other carries an inflated balloon on his head.

GUNMAN: I am going to perform the remarkable William Tell feat. I am going to shoot that apple from my assistant's head.

ASSISTANT: This isn't an apple. It's a balloon.

GUNMAN: Well, we will pretend it's an apple. And I am going to shoot it off your head.

ASSISTANT: Goodbye. (Starts to walk away – but the gunman catches him and brings him back to the centre of the stage.)

The assistant then begins to shake with fear. The gunman takes aim with his gun but has to keep the gun moving around a lot because the assistant is shaking so much.

GUNMAN: Keep still!

ASSISTANT: I can't. I'm nervous!

GUNMAN: There's no need to be nervous. I'm not nervous.

ASSISTANT: It's alright for you. There is no need for you to be nervous.

GUNMAN: Of course there is. I have never done this before.

ASSISTANT: Goodbye. (He walks off. Once again the performer manages to catch him in time and hauls him back to the centre of the stage.)

GUNMAN: (Aiming his gun at the balloon) I want you to count to three and then I'll fire.

ASSISTANT: One . . . two . . . two and a half . . .

GUNMAN: Three!

There is a loud bang (created on a tape recorder or by someone off stage). The balloon bursts and water floods all over the poor assistant.

The balloon is filled with water from a tap before the performance and the bursting is done by the assistant who holds a small pin in his hand throughout the performance. He simply sticks the pin into the balloon at the right moment.

The growing man

For this gag you will need a long coat and a large, floppy hat.

Stuff a pair of gloves with material or cotton wool and then sew them to the ends of the jacket sleeves.

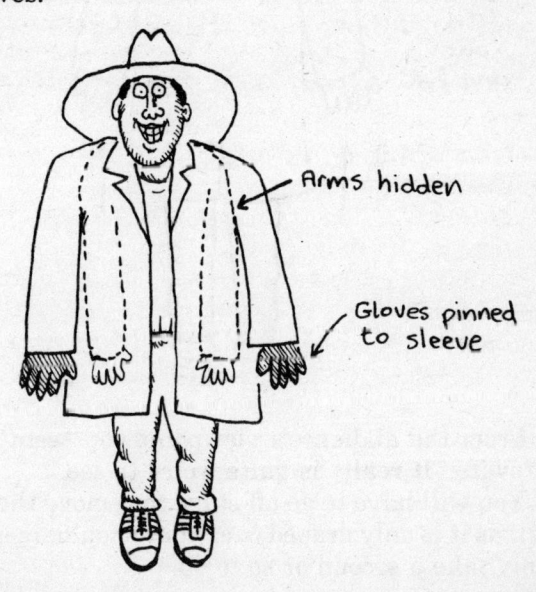

Put the coat over your shoulders and put the hat on so the back of it covers the coat collar.

From the front everything should appear normal. Your hands and arms are hidden under the front of the coat.

Turn your back to the audience.

Bring your hands up and grip the coat collar and the hat together.

Slowly lift your hands high in the air.

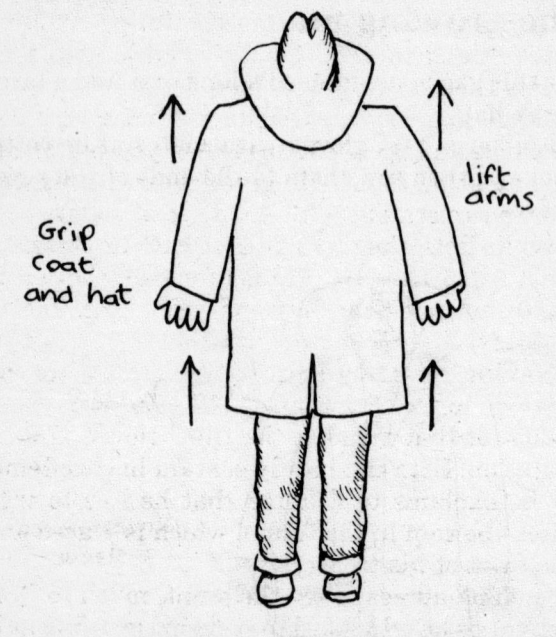

lift arms

Grip coat and hat

From the audience's viewpoint you seem to be growing. It really is quite weird to see.

You will have to go off stage to remove the coat but as it is only draped over your shoulders it will only take a second or so to do.

The catcher caught

This is a traditional gag used by clowns all over the world. Although most people have seen it many times, it still makes them laugh.

Three clowns are required to perform the gag. We will call them Alpha, Beta and Gamma.

Alpha challenges Beta to put a coin on his forehead and then make it drop into a funnel placed in the top of his trousers.

Beta accepts the bet and the funnel is put in place. He then puts his head back and Alpha places the coin on Beta's forehead.

'Don't do it yet,' says Alpha 'I'm just going to get a camera to take a photograph of you performing this amazing stunt.' He goes off and returns, not with a camera but with a bucket of water.

While Beta's head is still held back he cannot see what Alpha is doing. Alpha then pours water into the funnel and poor Beta ends up with rather wet trousers!

Having been caught himself, Beta is now anxious to try the stunt on someone else.

Just at that moment the third clown, Gamma, walks on. Beta can hardly contain his excitement as he explains to Gamma that he has to try to catch the coin in the funnel which is placed down the front of his trousers.

Gamma agrees to try the stunt, much to Beta's delight as he tries hard to stifle his giggling at the prospect of Gamma getting a soaking.

The coin is put in position and Beta rushes off to get the 'camera'. He returns with a bucket and pours water into the funnel – but nothing happens!

Gamma allows the coin to drop from his forehead (it doesn't matter whether it goes into the funnel or not) and removes the funnel from his trousers.

Beta is at a loss to understand why Gamma is not soaked. Gamma then reaches down the front of his trousers and removes a hot water bottle!

This stunt should only be performed where it will not matter if water goes on the floor.

Care must be taken when placing the funnel into the third clown's trousers. It must go into the hidden hot water bottle otherwise he will receive a soaking too!

The gag can also be performed with just two clowns by cutting out the first part (the soaking). In this case the second clown wins the bet and it is only when the first clown sadly wanders off (having lost his money) that the second clown reveals the hot water bottle.

The thing

On a table in the centre of the stage is a large box.

When you notice the box you are naturally curious about its contents. You look to one side of the stage and then to the other to make sure no one is watching. then you creep over to the box. Another quick look around and then you open the lid.

As soon as the lid is opened a white 'thing' leaps from the box and off to the side of the stage!

When the audience has finished laughing you look into the box once again.

This time the 'thing' flies from the other side of the stage into the box!

This takes a bit of setting up but it certainly gets a laugh.

The 'things' are actually two pieces of white cloth attached to lengths of black cord elastic. The first 'thing' is in the box and the elastic stretched to the side of the stage, where it is held by an assistant.

As soon as the box is opened the elastic pulls the 'thing' from the box and off the stage.

The second 'thing' works in reverse. An assistant on the other side of the stage holds the 'thing' and the other end of the elastic is fixed to the inside of the box.

When you open the box for the second time the assistant releases the 'thing' and the elastic pulls it into the box.

Flower power

In your left lapel you have a beautiful flower. During your act you decide to smell the flower so you remove it from your lapel and take a good sniff.

You hold the flower out to the right of your body as you admire its beauty.

When you let go of the flower it leaps back to your buttonhole!

The flower (an artificial one) is attached to a thread. The thread goes through the material of your coat and runs down to a weight suspended inside the coat.

The weight holds the flower in place against your lapel.

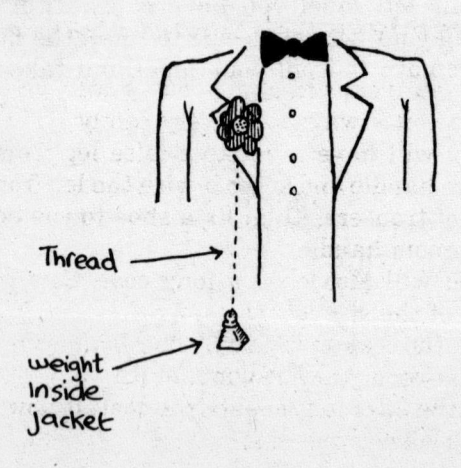

When you remove the flower from your lapel, you hold it out to the full extent of the thread. When you let go of the flower, the weight pulls the thread and the flower back into place.

Button up

You take a button from your coat and look at it for a moment or two.

When you release your hold on the button it jumps back to its normal position.

This works in exactly the same way as the **Flower Power** trick. A weight and a thread work the stunt for you.

You could also work **Flower Power** and **Button Up** using a length of black cord elastic in place of the thread and weight.

Three legs are better than two

This is a very old gag – but it still gets laughs because it always looks very funny.

You will have to make a false leg from an old broom handle and cover it with the leg from an old pair of trousers. Then fix a shoe to the bottom of the broom handle.

You will also need a long coat. Sew gloves to each of the sleeves, as shown.

Put the coat on with only one arm in the sleeves, as shown in the drawing. With your free hand, hold the false leg beneath the coat. It now looks as if you have three legs.

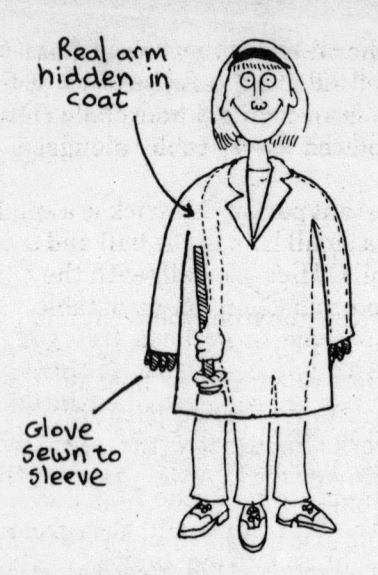

Step forward with the left leg and move the false leg forward at the same time.

Move the right leg forward between the first two and then continue this movement across the stage.

This looks extremely funny and, with practice, you will soon devise several other funny looking movements using the false leg.

A glass of milk

Halfway through your act you pretend to feel rather thirsty. The problem is solved quite simply.

You take a rubber glove and blow it up so the inflated fingers look rather like a cow's udder, which you then proceed to milk!

Much to everyone's surprise milk actually does

pour from the udder into a waiting glass! You then take a sip of milk and carry on with your act!

The glove is an ordinary household rubber glove which is placed on a table alongside a glass tumbler.

The important part of this trick is a small rubber ball. Make a small hole in the ball and then fill the ball with milk. Hide the ball (with the hole uppermost) behind something on your table.

When you come to perform this gag, pick up the glove with one hand and, at the same time, secretly pick up the rubber ball in the other hand.

Blow up the glove then bring your other hand (holding the concealed ball) up to one of the fingers. Pretend to milk the finger whilst really squeezing the ball. Milk will flow from the ball and into the glass on your table.

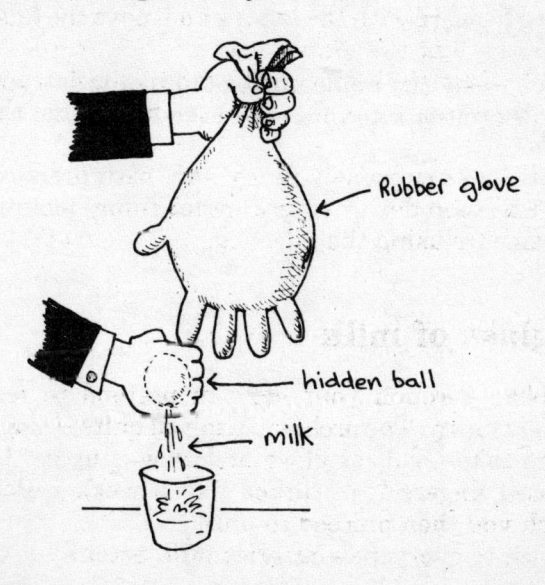

Glass of water gag

You will need three people on stage to perfom this gag.

The first person drinks a glass of water.

The second person tilts his head back and gargles.

The third person spits water from his mouth into a bucket he is holding.

The only preparation needed for this gag is that persons two and three have a mouthful of water before they go on stage.

Nothing needs to be said to emphasize the gag. Just go through the motions as described above and your audience will have a good laugh.

Tail seat

If you play the piano and would like to introduce some comedy into your act you could try this trick.

You will need to wear a man's tail coat. As tail coats can prove quite expensive, it is well worth while looking around jumble sales and markets for a suitable coat for this gag.

Slip an L-shaped board into the tails of the coat as shown.

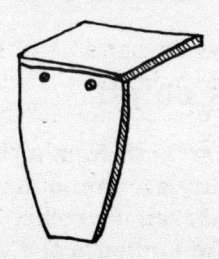

When you walk on stage to play the piano there is no stool for you to sit on.

Show that this does not bother you and approach the piano and sit down – on your coat tails!

COMEDY PROPS

Toothless comb

Remove all the teeth from a comb.

During your act announce that you have invented a marvellous comb, especially for bald men. Show the audience the toothless comb and then run it over your head as if combing your hair.

Like many sight gags, this may not sound funny in print, but just try it and you will have your audience laughing.

Big head

Part way through your act you decide to comb your hair. You pick up a comb from your table but it is gigantic!

You do not have to say anything – just pretend to comb your hair and then replace the comb on your table. The sight of the large comb will certainly bring a smile to the faces of your audience.

You can buy large combs from joke shops but you could easily make one from a sheet of thick card or plywood.

Ear, ear

Join two small boxes together with a long strip of cardboard.

The length of the cardboard should be such that when you place it on your head the boxes fit over your ears.

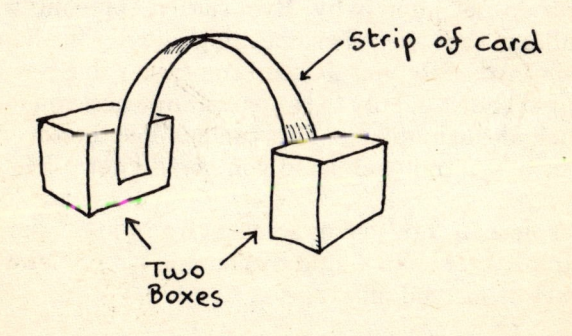

Put this on and walk on stage. Say something like: 'I don't know what I said to insult my mother . . . but she's just boxed my ears!'

← Boxed ears

Spot the spider

As you are performing your act, a large spider slowly descends on a thread above your head.

When the audience begins to laugh you pretend you do not know why. Eventually, someone will call out that there is something above your head. Immediately you look up the spider disappears out of sight . . . only to return again when you look back at the audience. This can be repeated several times . . . and each time you should get a bigger laugh.

You can buy joke spiders from joke shops. Simply tie one to a long thread and get a friend to work it for you off stage.

Coat hanger discomfort

Part way through your act you start fidgeting as if the collar of your coat is irritating you.

Eventually, you reach up to your collar and pull out a coat hanger.

Throw the coat hanger away and do not mention it at all. Just carry on with the rest of your act.

Sock it to 'em

Wear two socks of contrasting colours. You could, for example, put a red sock on your right foot and a blue sock on your left foot.

Part way through your act hitch up your trousers a little to show the contrasting socks.

Say: 'Do you like the socks? . . . I've got another pair exactly like them at home.'

The missing finger

During your act, or when you finish, put on a pair of gloves.

As you do this, bend one finger of the right hand so it does not go into the finger of the glove.

You look at your gloved hands and suddenly realize there is one finger missing!

Wiggle the empty glove finger back and forth to emphasize the fact that it is empty.

Remove the gloves in a panic and quickly count your fingers. When you see they are all intact, heave a great sigh of relief.

Long arms

This is a good gag for a singer — or at any point in your act where you may decide to sing a song.

As you are singing, wave your arms around in time to the music. Gradually your arms get longer . . . and longer . . . and longer . . . and longer!

You will need to make (or ask your mother to make) a jacket with especially long sleeves for this gag. Place a stick into each sleeve and on the end of each stick, attach a stuffed glove.

When you put the jacket on, hold the end of each stick in your hands. At this point you should try to keep your 'arms' as short as possible.

As you wave your arms about while singing, gradually extend your real arms to their full length — and it appears they are growing all the time!

Matching handkerchief

When you come on stage you have a handkerchief in the top pocket of your jacket.

As you are a very smart person the handkerchief matches your tie — but it soons becomes obvious, when you try to pull the handkerchief out, that it really is the end of your tie which passes through a slit in the bottom of your pocket.

Ask your mother to make the slit in the pocket for you, or at least check what you are doing, so it is done properly and with her knowledge.

Pull your socks up!

Part way through your act you realize that one of your socks needs pulling up.

You bend down and pull up the sock and it is pulled up your leg!

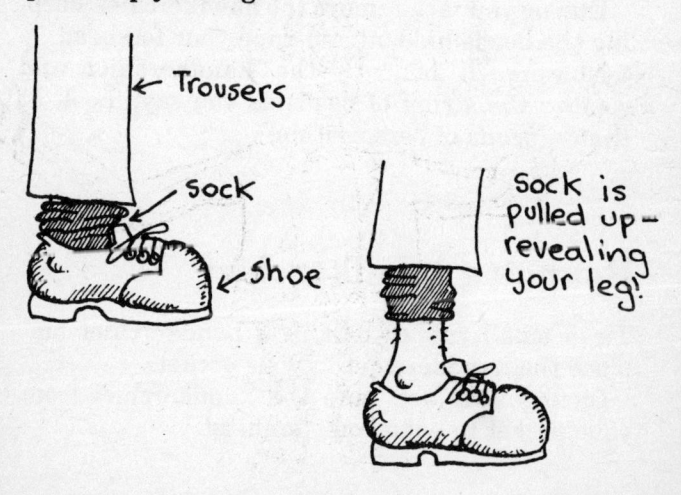

The sock is worn in the normal way but the whole of the foot section has been cut off so you are wearing just a tube of wool around your leg as shown.

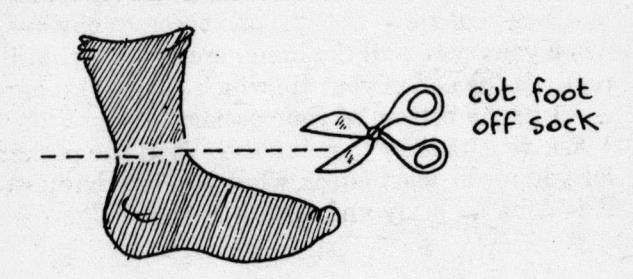

cut foot off sock

Beads of perspiration

Wrap a string of beads in a handkerchief and put the handkerchief in your pocket.

During your act, remove the handkerchief (keeping the beads hidden) and wipe your forehead.

Now reach beneath the handkerchief and remove the string of beads as you say: 'Look at that – *beads* of perspiration!'

Bouncing handkerchief

Tie a small rubber ball in a handkerchief and place the handkerchief in your pocket.

During your act, take the handkerchief from your pocket to wipe your forehead.

Throw the handkerchief to the floor and catch it as it bounces.

Place the handkerchief back in your pocket without saying a word, as if a bouncing handkerchief was the most normal thing in the world!

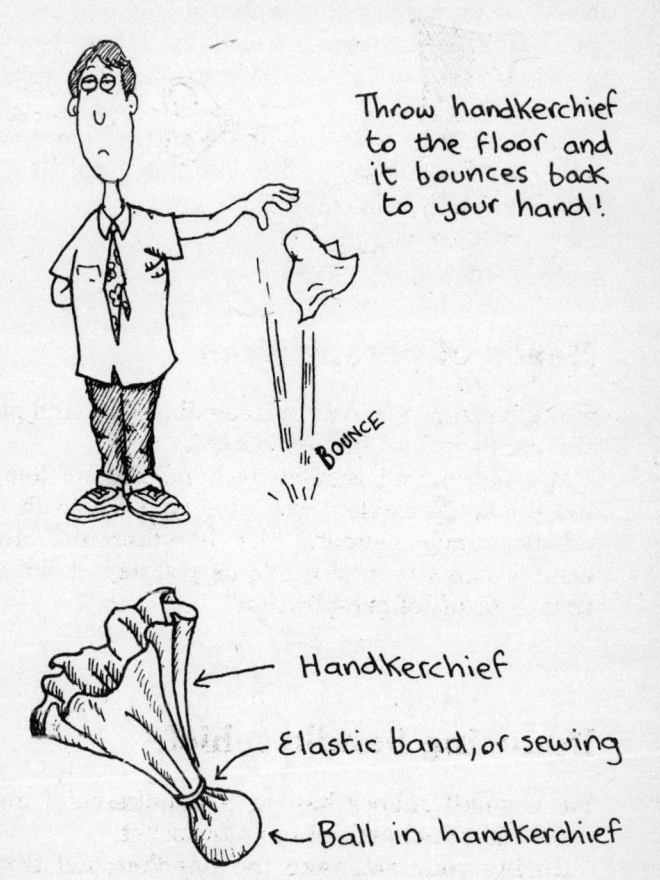

Throw handkerchief to the floor and it bounces back to your hand!

BOUNCE

Handkerchief

Elastic band, or sewing

Ball in handkerchief

A splitting headache

Make an arrow from cardboard like the one shown. A double strip of card at the centre lets the arrow be placed over your head. This central loop should be as narrow as possible so you can comb your hair over it to hide it from view. It now looks as if you have an arrow sticking through your head.

Walk on stage with the arrow in position and say: 'I don't know why, but I've got a splitting headache today.'

Arrow made of card

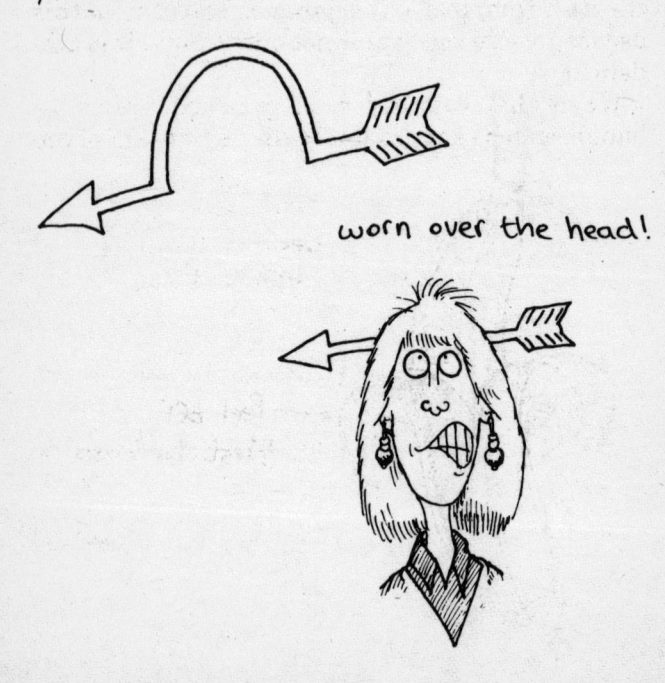

worn over the head!

Banana split

As you have been performing for a while you get a little hungry — so you decide to have a banana.

You peel the banana — but much to your surprise, and to the amusement of your audience, there is another banana inside! You have to peel the second banana before you can enjoy your well-earned snack.

The banana is prepared as follows:

First take a large banana and start to peel it from the top. Peel it carefully and for only about three centimetres from the top.

Now take a long, narrow dessert spoon and scoop the fruit from inside the banana. You can eat this as you go — so this gag is not only funny, it is also delicious!

When the fruit has been removed a smaller banana can be slipped inside the empty skin of the first. A small piece of transparent tape is used to hold the top end of the outer skin in place.

All you have to do now is pick up the banana during your act. Peel off the first banana to reveal the inner banana. Peel the second banana and take a good bite.

Light-headed

One performer has a light bulb attached to the top of his head with a simple cardboard frame like the one shown.

Light bulb held by holes in strips.

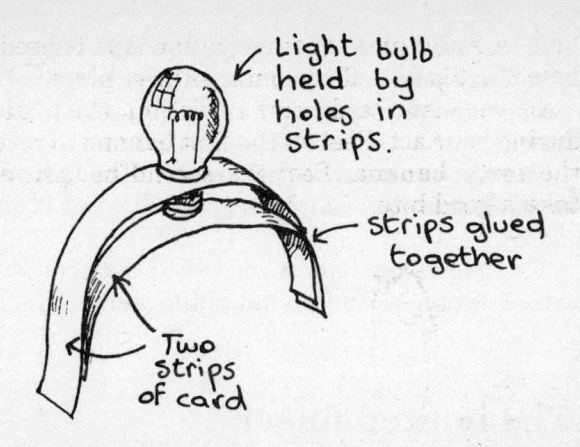

strips glued together

Two strips of card

The second performer spots the light bulb and asks: 'What's the matter with you?'

'Take no notice,' says the first 'I'm a bit light-headed today.'

Ball point

To make this prop you need a ball-point pen and a solid rubber ball.

Make a hole in the ball and push the point of the pen into it.

Biro

Ball

It is a good idea actually to glue it in place. But be careful what glue you use. Some glues dissolve rubber and you may end up with a gooey, gluey mess!

Show your audience the pen with the ball stuck on it. Just say: 'A ball-point pen,' and put it down again.

The gag takes only a second to perform but it gets a laugh — and it's laughter you're after.

The injured finger

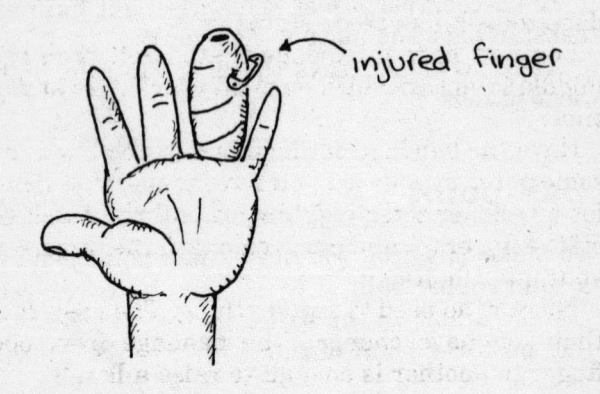

injured finger

Take a small piece of card and roll it around your finger. Use a piece of sticky tape to hold it together.

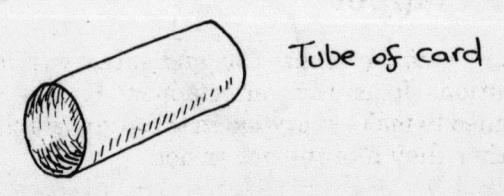

Tube of card

Put the tube on your finger and then wrap a bandage around it. Make the bandage quite thick and then use a large safety pin to secure the end.

covered with bandage and held in place by a large safety pin

If you wish, you can put some red ink on the bandage to look like blood stains.

You now have a bandage that is hollow in the middle so you can slip it on or off your finger at any time.

Have the bandage on the finger of one hand. At some point in your act you have to use that hand for a trick, or some juggling, so pull the bandage off the finger ... and put it on one of the fingers of your other hand!

There is no need to say anything. The mere fact that you have changed the bandage from one finger to another is enough to raise a laugh.

Autoclapper

During your act show the audience your latest invention. It is the autoclapper. It has been designed to make everyone in the audience clap — whether they like the act or not.

Your assistant then comes on wearing the autoclapper. This consists of a pair of gloves (which your assistant is wearing) joined together with a metal spring.

Your assistant goes through the actions of clapping automatically (as if controlled by the spring) and your audience will have a good laugh.

Playing cards

For this prop you will need a small block of wood. This must be exactly the same size and shape as a pack of playing cards.

You will also need a small mouth organ and two real playing cards.

Cut a small piece out of the block of wood, large enough to hold the mouth organ.

Put the mouth organ into the cut-out section and glue a playing card on the top and the bottom of the block.

Use a black felt-tipped pen to draw lines around the outer edges of the block. If you do this properly

Real card on top and bottom

Block of wood covered with black lines

mouth organ hidden in block

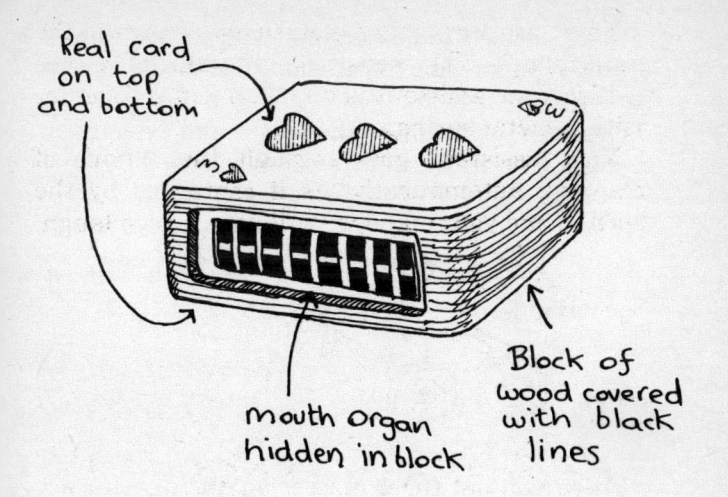

the completed item should look exactly like an ordinary pack of cards.

During your act pick up this 'pack of cards', blow into the mouth organ and say: 'Playing cards'.

Another quick performing gag, but it gets a laugh!

The eyes have it

You need an old pair of plastic sunglasses to make this prop.

old pair of sunglasses

Draw some funny looking eyes on two small pieces of paper. The paper should be the same size as the lenses on the glasses.

Glue the papers on to the lenses and then make a small hole in the centre of each lens.

When you put these glasses on during your act your audience will laugh like crazy.

Why the holes in the lenses? So you can see what you are doing, of course!

Other great reads from Red Fox

Further Red Fox titles that you might enjoy reading are listed on the following pages. They are available in bookshops or they can be ordered directly from us.

If you would like to order books, please send this form and the money due to:

ARROW BOOKS, BOOKSERVICE BY POST, PO BOX 29, DOUGLAS, ISLE OF MAN, BRITISH ISLES. Please enclose a cheque or postal order made out to Arrow Books Ltd for the amount due, plus 22p per book for postage and packing, both for orders within the UK and for overseas orders.

NAME _____

ADDRESS _____

_____

Please print clearly.

Whilst every effort is made to keep prices low, it is sometimes necessary to increase cover prices at short notice. If you are ordering books by post, to save delay it is advisable to phone to confirm the correct price. The number to ring is THE SALES DEPARTMENT 071 (if outside London) 973 9700.

*Other great reads from **Red Fox***

The latest and funniest joke books are from Red Fox!

THE OZONE FRIENDLY JOKE BOOK
Kim Harris, Chris Langham, Robert Lee, Richard Turner

What's green and highly dangerous?
How do you start a row between conservationists?
What's green and can't be rubbed out?

Green jokes for green people (non-greens will be pea-green when they see how hard you're laughing), bags and bags of them (biodegradable of course).

All the jokes in this book are printed on environmentally friendly paper and every copy you buy will help GREENPEACE save our planet.

* David Bellamy with a machine gun.
* Pour oil on troubled waters.
* The Indelible hulk.

ISBN 0 09 973190 8 £1.99

THE HAUNTED HOUSE JOKE BOOK
John Hegarty

There are skeletons in the scullery . . .
Beasties in the bath . . .
There are spooks in the sitting room
And jokes to make you laugh . . .

Search your home and see if we are right. Then come back, sit down and shudder to the hauntingly funny and eerily rib-rattling jokes in this book.

ISBN 0 09 9621509 £1.99

Other great reads from **Red Fox**

Discover the wide range of exciting activity books from Red Fox

THE PAINT AND PRINT FUN BOOK
Steve and Megumi Biddle

Would you like to make a glittering bird? A colourful tiger? A stained-glass window? Or an old treasure map? Well, all you need are ordinary materials like vegetables, tinfoil, paper doilies, even your own fingers to make all kinds of amazing things—without too much mess.

Follow Steve and Megumi's step-by-step instructions and clear diagrams and you can make all kinds of professional designs—to hang on your wall or give to your friends.

ISBN 0 09 9644606   £2.50

CRAZY KITES   Peter Eldin

This book is a terrific introduction to the art of flying kites. There are lots of easy-to-assemble, different kites to make, from the basic flat kite to the Chinese dragon and the book also gives you clear instructions on launching, flying and landing. Kite flying is fun. Help yourself to a soaring good time.

ISBN 0 09 964550 5   £2.50

Other great reads from **Red Fox**

CRAZY PAINTING   Juliet Bawden

There are loads of imaginative ideas and suggstions in this easy-to-follow activity book all about painting. First it teaches you the basics: how to make your own vegetable dyes, mix paints, create a fabulous marbled effect and decorate ceramics. Then the fun begins. You can design your own curtains, make zany brooches for your friends, create your own colourful wrapping paper and amaze your family with hours of painting pleasure.

ISBN 0 09 954320 6   £2.25

DRESSING UP FUN   Terry Burrows

Dressing up is always fun—for a party, a play or just for a laugh! In Dressing Up Fun you'll find loads of ideas for all kinds of costumes and make-up. So whether you'd like to be a cowboy, punk or witch, superman, a princess or the Empire State Building, youll find them all in this book.

ISBN 0 09 965110 6   £2.99